HANDWRITING
LEARN TO
PRINT!

PETER PAUPER PRESS, INC.
White Plains, New York

PETER PAUPER PRESS

In 1928, at the age of twenty-two, Peter Beilenson began printing books on a small press in the basement of his parents' home in Larchmont, New York. Peter—and later, his wife, Edna—sought to create fine books that sold at "prices even a pauper could afford."

Today, still family owned and operated, Peter Pauper Press continues to honor our founders' legacy of quality, value, and fun for big kids and small kids alike.

Designed by Margaret Rubiano

Copyright © 2015
Peter Pauper Press, Inc.
Manufactured for Peter Pauper Press, Inc.
202 Mamaroneck Avenue
White Plains, NY, USA 10601
All rights reserved
ISBN 978-1-4413-1816-9
Printed in China

Published in the United Kingdom and Europe by
Peter Pauper Press, Inc. c/o White Pebble International
Unit 2, Plot 11 Terminus Road
Chichester, West Sussex PO19 8TX, UK

14 13 12 11 10

Visit us at www.peterpauper.com

· · · · · · · · · · · INTRODUCTION · · · · · · · · · · ·

This book helps children teach themselves how to print, or lets them refine the skills they already have. With helpful diagrams, plenty of space to write in, and fun and simple exercises, this book is the perfect companion for beginning writers.

Learning to print helps children develop fine motor skills and writing things down helps them retain more information.

Here's what's inside:

LOWERCASE ALPHABET

a b c d e f

g h i j k l

m n o p q r

s t u v w x

y z

A B C D E F G H I J K L M N O P Q R S T U V W X Y Z
a b c d e f g h i j k l m n o p q r s t u v w x y z

CAPITAL
ALPHABET

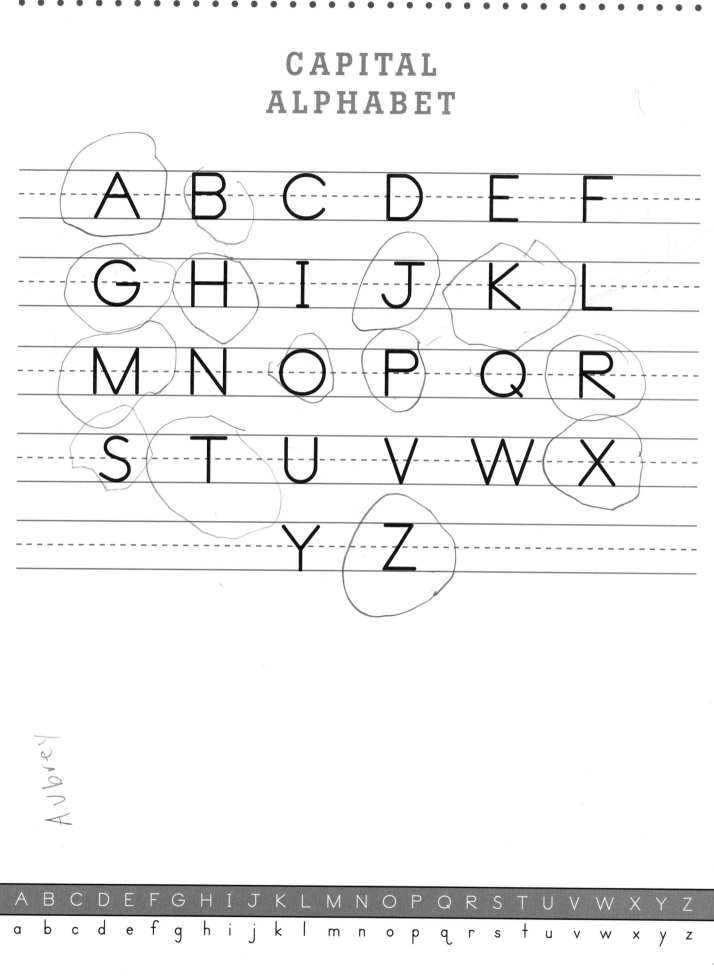

A B C D E F
G H I J K L
M N O P Q R
S T U V W X
Y Z

Aubrey

A B C D E F G H I J K L M N O P Q R S T U V W X Y Z
a b c d e f g h i j k l m n o p q r s t u v w x y z

Trace and write the letters below. The arrows show you where to begin.

a a a a a a a a a a

a a a a a a a a a a

A A A A A A

alligator

Trace and write the letters below. The arrows show you where to begin.

b   b   b   b   b

B   B   B   B   B

bees

A B C D E F G H I J K L M N O P Q R S T U V W X Y Z
a b c d e f g h i j k l m n o p q r s t u v w x y z

Trace and write the letters below. The arrows show you where to begin.

c   c   c   c   c   c

C   C   C   C   C   C

cat

A B C D E F G H I J K L M N O P Q R S T U V W X Y Z
a b c d e f g h i j k l m n o p q r s t u v w x y z

8

Trace and write the letters below. The arrows show you where to begin.

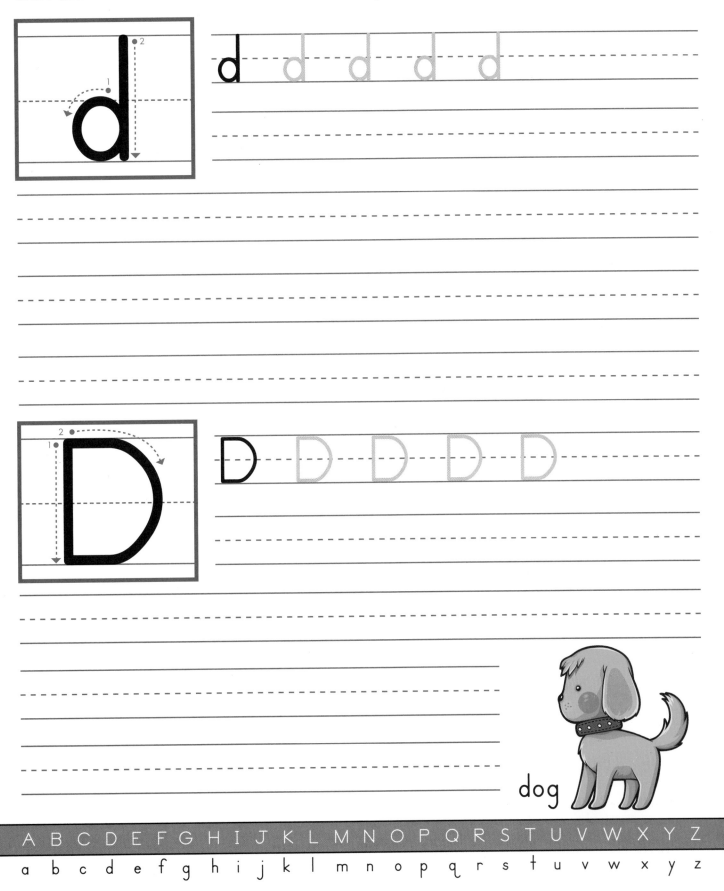

d   d   d   d   d

D   D   D   D   D

dog

A B C D E F G H I J K L M N O P Q R S T U V W X Y Z
a b c d e f g h i j k l m n o p q r s t u v w x y z

E

Trace and write the letters below. The arrows show you where to begin.

e e e e e

E E E E E E

elephant

A B C D E F G H I J K L M N O P Q R S T U V W X Y Z
a b c d e f g h i j k l m n o p q r s t u v w x y z

10

Trace and write the letters below. The arrows show you where to begin.

f f f f f

F F F F F F

fox

G

Trace and write the letters below. The arrows show you where to begin.

g g g g g

G G G G G G

giraffe

A B C D E F G H I J K L M N O P Q R S T U V W X Y Z
a b c d e f g h i j k l m n o p q r s t u v w x y z

12

Trace and write the letters below. The arrows show you where to begin.

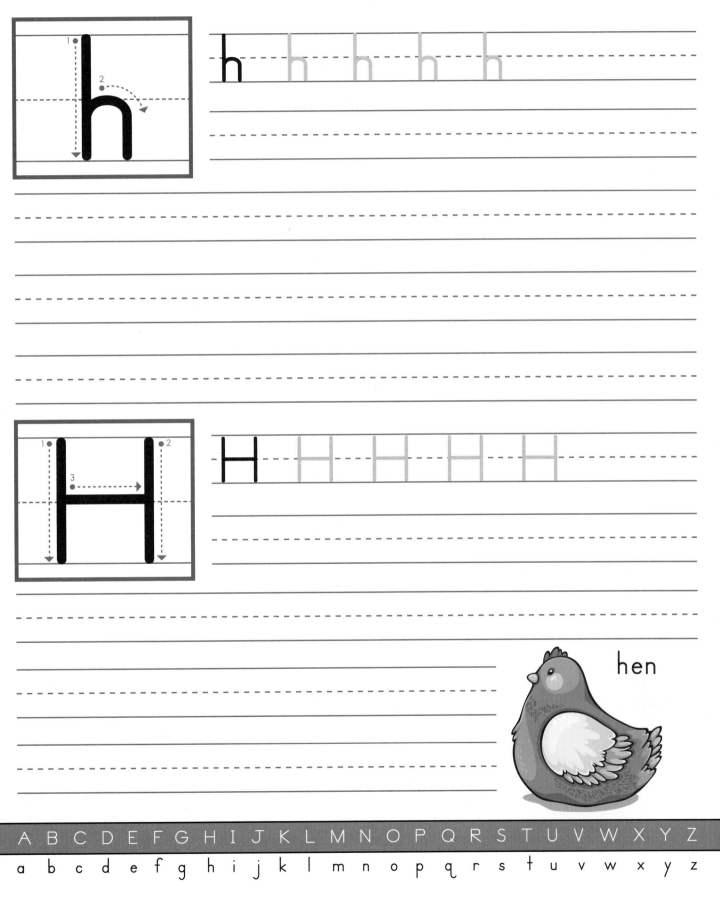

hen

Trace and write the letters below. The arrows show you where to begin.

i

I

ice cream

A B C D E F G H I J K L M N O P Q R S T U V W X Y Z
a b c d e f g h i j k l m n o p q r s t u v w x y z

Trace and write the letters below. The arrows show you where to begin.

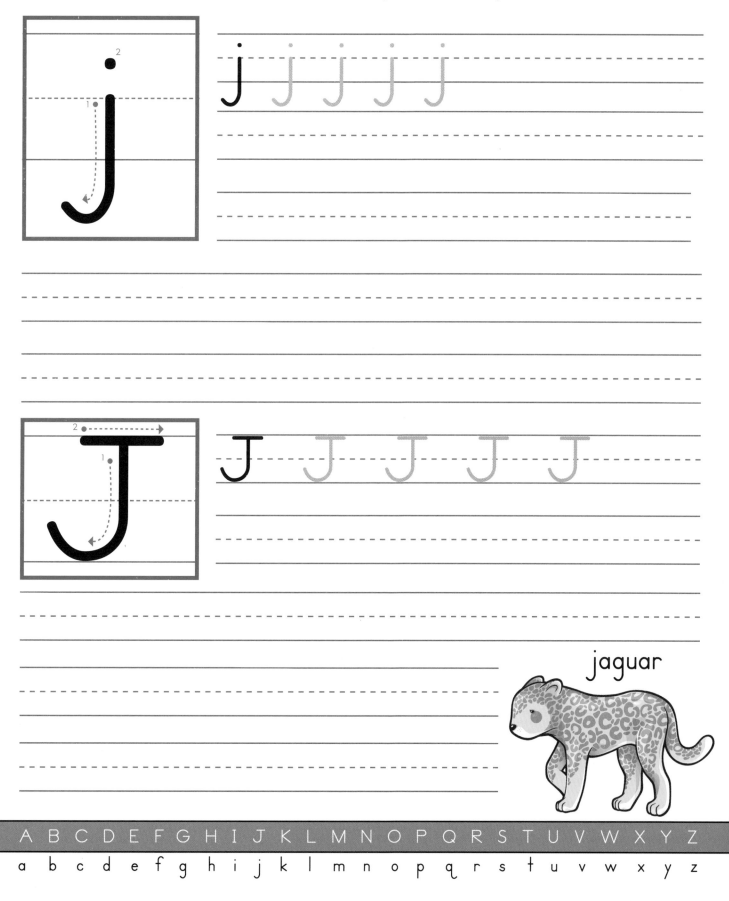

jaguar

A B C D E F G H I J K L M N O P Q R S T U V W X Y Z
a b c d e f g h i j k l m n o p q r s t u v w x y z

Trace and write the letters below. The arrows show you where to begin.

k   k   k   k   k   k

K   K   K   K   K   K

kangaroo

Trace and write the letters below. The arrows show you where to begin.

lamb

A B C D E F G H I J K L M N O P Q R S T U V W X Y Z

a b c d e f g h i j k l m n o p q r s t u v w x y z

Trace and write the letters below. The arrows show you where to begin.

m   m   m   m   m

M   M   M   M   M

monkey

A B C D E F G H I J K L M N O P Q R S T U V W X Y Z
a b c d e f g h i j k l m n o p q r s t u v w x y z

Trace and write the letters below. The arrows show you where to begin.

n n n n n

N N N N N

nest

A B C D E F G H I J K L M N O P Q R S T U V W X Y Z

a b c d e f g h i j k l m n o p q r s t u v w x y z

Trace and write the letters below. The arrows show you where to begin.

O o o o o o

O

o o o o o o

octopus

P

Trace and write the letters below. The arrows show you where to begin.

p p p p p

P P P P P

pear

A B C D E F G H I J K L M N O P Q R S T U V W X Y Z
a b c d e f g h i j k l m n o p q r s t u v w x y z

21

Q

Trace and write the letters below. The arrows show you where to begin.

q   q q q q q

Q   Q Q Q Q Q

quail

A B C D E F G H I J K L M N O P Q R S T U V W X Y Z
a b c d e f g h i j k l m n o p q r s t u v w x y z

22

Trace and write the letters below. The arrows show you where to begin.

r r r r r

R R R R R

rabbit

A B C D E F G H I J K L M N O P Q R S T U V W X Y Z

a b c d e f g h i j k l m n o p q r s t u v w x y z

Trace and write the letters below. The arrows show you where to begin.

s s s s s s

S S S S S S

sun

Trace and write the letters below. The arrows show you where to begin.

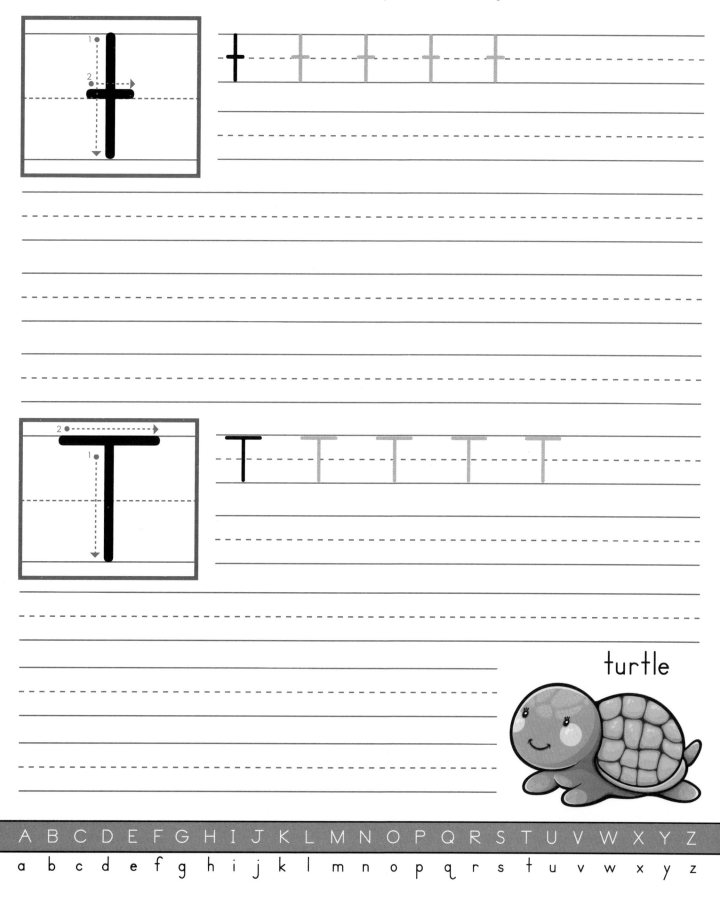

turtle

A B C D E F G H I J K L M N O P Q R S T U V W X Y Z

a b c d e f g h i j k l m n o p q r s t u v w x y z

Trace and write the letters below. The arrows show you where to begin.

u   u   u   u   u   u

U   U   U   U   U   U

unicorn

Trace and write the letters below. The arrows show you where to begin.

V V V V V

V V V V V

violin

W

Trace and write the letters below. The arrows show you where to begin.

W W W W W

W W W W W W

wolf

A B C D E F G H I J K L M N O P Q R S T U V W X Y Z
a b c d e f g h i j k l m n o p q r s t u v w x y z

Trace and write the letters below. The arrows show you where to begin.

X   X   X   X   X   X

X   X   X   X   X

xylophone

Trace and write the letters below. The arrows show you where to begin.

y y y y y

Y Y Y Y Y

yak

A B C D E F G H I J K L M N O P Q R S T U V W X Y Z
a b c d e f g h i j k l m n o p q r s t u v w x y z

Trace and write the letters below. The arrows show you where to begin.

z z z z z z

Z Z Z Z Z Z

zipper

A B C D E F G H I J K L M N O P Q R S T U V W X Y Z

a b c d e f g h i j k l m n o p q r s t u v w x y z

Trace and print each word.

Adam Adam

all all

ant ant

ate ate

as as

A B C D E F G H I J K L M N O P Q R S T U V W X Y Z
a b c d e f g h i j k l m n o p q r s t u v w x y z

Trace and print each word.

bat   bat

Bert   Bert

big   big

blue   blue

by   by

A B C D E F G H I J K L M N O P Q R S T U V W X Y Z
a b c d e f g h i j k l m n o p q r s t u v w x y z

Trace and print each word.

cat   cat

Chuck   Chuck

cone   cone

cub   cub

cute   cute

A B C D E F G H I J K L M N O P Q R S T U V W X Y Z

a b c d e f g h i j k l m n o p q r s t u v w x y z

Trace and print each word.

Dad Dad

dig dig

dog dog

dry dry

duck duck

A B C D E F G H I J K L M N O P Q R S T U V W X Y Z
a b c d e f g h i j k l m n o p q r s t u v w x y z

Trace and print each word.

eat eat

eel eel

Evan Evan

extra extra

each each

A B C D E F G H I J K L M N O P Q R S T U V W X Y Z
a b c d e f g h i j k l m n o p q r s t u v w x y z

Trace and print each word.

find find

Fiona Fiona

frog frog

fun fun

for for

A B C D E F G H I J K L M N O P Q R S T U V W X Y Z
a b c d e f g h i j k l m n o p q r s t u v w x y z

Trace and print each word.

game   game

Gina   Gina

goat   goat

green   green

get   get

A B C D E F G H I J K L M N O P Q R S T U V W X Y Z
a b c d e f g h i j k l m n o p q r s t u v w x y z

Trace and print each word.

hand hand

Herb Herb

hippo hippo

hug hug

happy happy

A B C D E F G H I J K L M N O P Q R S T U V W X Y Z
a b c d e f g h i j k l m n o p q r s t u v w x y z

Trace and print each word.

igloo igloo

into into

it it

Ireland Ireland

ice ice

A B C D E F G H I J K L M N O P Q R S T U V W X Y Z
a b c d e f g h i j k l m n o p q r s t u v w x y z

Trace and print each word.

Jake Jake

jam jam

job job

jump jump

jet jet

A B C D E F G H I J K L M N O P Q R S T U V W X Y Z
a b c d e f g h i j k l m n o p q r s t u v w x y z

Trace and print each word.

keep keep

kite kite

knot knot

Kim Kim

key key

A B C D E F G H I J K L M N O P Q R S T U V W X Y Z

a b c d e f g h i j k l m n o p q r s t u v w x y z

Trace and print each word.

land land

Leo Leo

lion lion

log log

luck luck

A B C D E F G H I J K L M N O P Q R S T U V W X Y Z

a b c d e f g h i j k l m n o p q r s t u v w x y z

Trace and print each word.

map   map

meet   meet

Mom   Mom

moon   moon

mug   mug

A B C D E F G H I J K L M N O P Q R S T U V W X Y Z
a b c d e f g h i j k l m n o p q r s t u v w x y z

Trace and print each word.

name name

new new

Nile Nile

nose nose

number number

A B C D E F G H I J K L M N O P Q R S T U V W X Y Z
a b c d e f g h i j k l m n o p q r s t u v w x y z

Trace and print each word.

off off

Otis Otis

old old

owl owl

oxen oxen

A B C D E F G H I J K L M N O P Q R S T U V W X Y Z
a b c d e f g h i j k l m n o p q r s t u v w x y z

46

Trace and print each word.

Paris Paris

play play

pig pig

pop pop

pen pen

A B C D E F G H I J K L M N O P Q R S T U V W X Y Z

a b c d e f g h i j k l m n o p q r s t u v w x y z

Trace and print each word.

Quinn Quinn

quack quack

queen queen

quiet quiet

quick quick

A B C D E F G H I J K L M N O P Q R S T U V W X Y Z

a b c d e f g h i j k l m n o p q r s t u v w x y z

Trace and print each word.

red red

rock rock

run run

Ryan Ryan

rat rat

A B C D E F G H I J K L M N O P Q R S T U V W X Y Z

a b c d e f g h i j k l m n o p q r s t u v w x y z

Trace and print each word.

Sam Sam

six six

stop stop

sun sun

said said

A B C D E F G H I J K L M N O P Q R S T U V W X Y Z
a b c d e f g h i j k l m n o p q r s t u v w x y z

Trace and print each word.

Tara   Tara

tree   tree

tub   tub

two   two

top   top

A B C D E F G H I J K L M N O P Q R S T U V W X Y Z
a b c d e f g h i j k l m n o p q r s t u v w x y z

U

Trace and print each word.

ugly ugly

under under

us us

Uma Uma

up up

A B C D E F G H I J K L M N O P Q R S T U V W X Y Z
a b c d e f g h i j k l m n o p q r s t u v w x y z

52

V

Trace and print each word.

van   van

Vera   Vera

very   very

visit   visit

vat   vat

A B C D E F G H I J K L M N O P Q R S T U V W X Y Z
a b c d e f g h i j k l m n o p q r s t u v w x y z

53

Trace and print each word.

Wally Wally

water water

win win

worm worm

when when

A B C D E F G H I J K L M N O P Q R S T U V W X Y Z
a b c d e f g h i j k l m n o p q r s t u v w x y z

Trace and print each word.

box   box

mix   mix

exit   exit

X-ray   X-ray

text   text

A B C D E F G H I J K L M N O P Q R S T U V W X Y Z
a b c d e f g h i j k l m n o p q r s t u v w x y z

Y

Trace and print each word.

yarn   yarn

yellow   yellow

Yoshi   Yoshi

you   you

yeti   yeti

A B C D E F G H I J K L M N O P Q R S T U V W X Y Z
a b c d e f g h i j k l m n o p q r s t u v w x y z

56

Trace and print each word.

zebra zebra

zip zip

Zoe Zoe

zoo zoo

zero zero

A B C D E F G H I J K L M N O P Q R S T U V W X Y Z
a b c d e f g h i j k l m n o p q r s t u v w x y z

Trace and write the sentence.

Ants are awake.

Ants are awake.

Trace and write the sentence.

Bees buzz by.

Bees buzz by.

A B C D E F G H I J K L M N O P Q R S T U V W X Y Z
a b c d e f g h i j k l m n o p q r s t u v w x y z

Trace and write the sentence.

Cute cubs climb.

Cute cubs climb.

A B C D E F G H I J K L M N O P Q R S T U V W X Y Z

a b c d e f g h i j k l m n o p q r s t u v w x y z

Trace and write the sentence.

Dogs dig deep.

Dogs dig deep.

A B C D E F G H I J K L M N O P Q R S T U V W X Y Z
a b c d e f g h i j k l m n o p q r s t u v w x y z

61

Trace and write the sentence.

Electric eels eat.

Electric eels eat.

A B C D E F G H I J K L M N O P Q R S T U V W X Y Z
a b c d e f g h i j k l m n o p q r s t u v w x y z

Trace and write the sentence.

Fairies fly far.

Fairies fly far.

Trace and write the sentence.

Green goop glows.

Green goop glows.

A B C D E F G H I J K L M N O P Q R S T U V W X Y Z

a b c d e f g h i j k l m n o p q r s t u v w x y z

64

Trace and write the sentence.

Hippos hop heavily.

Hippos hop heavily.

A B C D E F G H I J K L M N O P Q R S T U V W X Y Z
a b c d e f g h i j k l m n o p q r s t u v w x y z

Trace and write the sentence.

It is I.

It is I.

Trace and write the sentence.

Jason jumps.

Jason jumps.

Trace and write the sentence.

Kings keep keys.

Kings keep keys.

Trace and write the sentence.

Leaves land lightly.

Leaves land lightly.

A B C D E F G H I J K L M N O P Q R S T U V W X Y Z
a b c d e f g h i j k l m n o p q r s t u v w x y z

Trace and write the sentence.

Michael moves.

Michael moves.

Trace and write the sentence.

Newts nap nicely.

Newts nap nicely.

A B C D E F G H I J K L M N O P Q R S T U V W X Y Z
a b c d e f g h i j k l m n o p q r s t u v w x y z

Trace and write the sentence.

Owen's owl is out.

Owen's owl is out.

Trace and write the sentence.

Pigs play ping-pong.

Pigs play ping-pong.

A B C D E F G H I J K L M N O P Q R S T U V W X Y Z
a b c d e f g h i j k l m n o p q r s t u v w x y z

Trace and write the sentence.

Quack quickly.

Quack quickly.

Trace and write the sentence.

Ravens roost.

Ravens roost.

Trace and write the sentence.

Sloths sleep soundly.

Sloths sleep soundly.

A B C D E F G H I J K L M N O P Q R S T U V W X Y Z
a b c d e f g h i j k l m n o p q r s t u v w x y z

T

Trace and write the sentence.

Toads take tea.

Toads take tea.

A B C D E F G H I J K L M N O P Q R S T U V W X Y Z

a b c d e f g h i j k l m n o p q r s t u v w x y z

77

Trace and write the sentence.

Use Upton's umbrella.

Use Upton's umbrella.

A B C D E F G H I J K L M N O P Q R S T U V W X Y Z
a b c d e f g h i j k l m n o p q r s t u v w x y z

Trace and write the sentence.

Visit vast valleys.

Visit vast valleys.

A B C D E F G H I J K L M N O P Q R S T U V W X Y Z

a b c d e f g h i j k l m n o p q r s t u v w x y z

Trace and write the sentence.

Worms wiggle.

Worms wiggle.

Trace and write the sentence.

Foxes fix X-rays.

Foxes fix X-rays.

A B C D E F G H I J K L M N O P Q R S T U V W X Y Z
a b c d e f g h i j k l m n o p q r s t u v w x y z

Trace and write the sentence.

Yaks yawn.

Yaks yawn.

A B C D E F G H I J K L M N O P Q R S T U V W X Y Z
a b c d e f g h i j k l m n o p q r s t u v w x y z

Trace and write the sentence.

Zebras zigzag.

Zebras zigzag.

Write each number and number word.

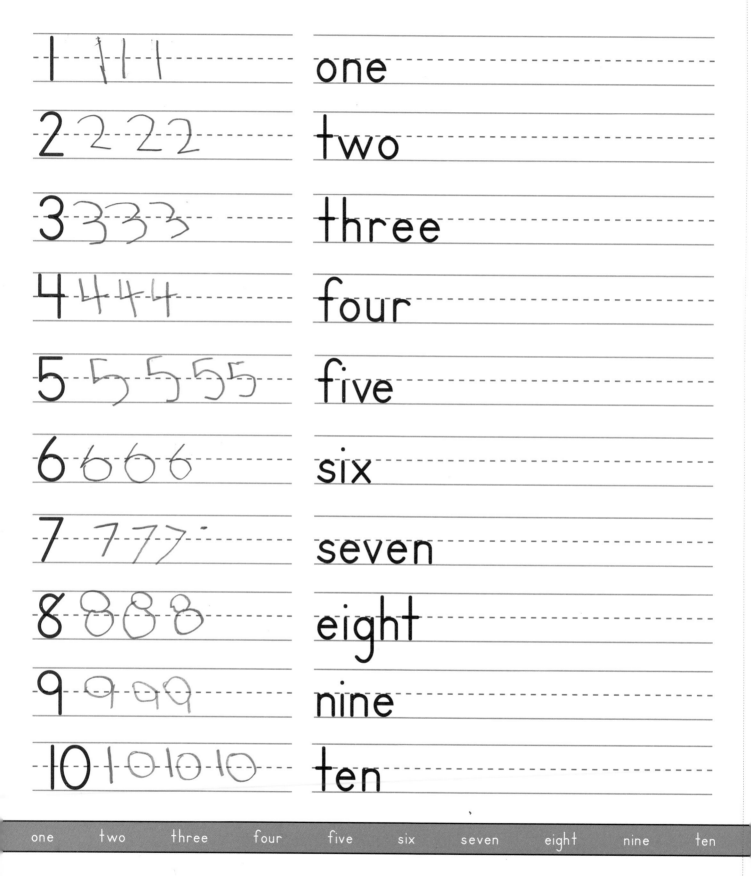

1 1 1 1   one

2 2 2 2   two

3 3 3 3   three

4 4 4 4   four

5 5 5 5 5   five

6 6 6 6   six

7 7 7 7   seven

8 8 8 8   eight

9 9 9 9   nine

10 10 10 10   ten

one   two   three   four   five   six   seven   eight   nine   ten

Write each day of the week.

Sunday

Friday

Monday

Saturday

Tuesday

Wednesday

Thursday

Sunday   Monday   Tuesday   Wednesday   Thursday   Friday   Saturday

Write each month of the year.

January

February

March

April

May

June

January   February   March   April   May   June

July

August

September

October

November

December

Print your name on the lines below.

A B C D E F G H I J K L M N O P Q R S T U V W X Y Z
a b c d e f g h i j k l m n o p q r s t u v w x y z

Here are pictures of things A to Z. Can you print the word that goes with each picture? You'll find the words printed on pages 95 and 96.

ant

bees

cat

dolphin

A B C D E F G H I J K L M N O P Q R S T U V W X Y Z

a b c d e f g h i j k l m n o p q r s t u v w x y z

Can you print the word that goes with each picture? You'll find the words printed on pages 95 and 96.

elephant

fox

goose

horse

A B C D E F G H I J K L M N O P Q R S T U V W X Y Z

a b c d e f g h i j k l m n o p q r s t u v w x y z

Can you print the word that goes with each picture? You'll find the words printed on pages 95 and 96.

iguana

jellyfish

koala

lamb

moon

A B C D E F G H I J K L M N O P Q R S T U V W X Y Z

a b c d e f g h i j k l m n o p q r s t u v w x y z

Can you print the word that goes with each picture? You'll find the words printed on pages 95 and 96.

nest

owl

pig

queen

A B C D E F G H I J K L M N O P Q R S T U V W X Y Z
a b c d e f g h i j k l m n o p q r s t u v w x y z

Can you print the word that goes with each picture? You'll find the words printed on pages 95 and 96.

radish

sheep

turtle

unicorn

A B C D E F G H I J K L M N O P Q R S T U V W X Y Z

a b c d e f g h i j k l m n o p q r s t u v w x y z

Can you print the word that goes with each picture? You'll find the words printed on pages 95 and 96.

vulture

whale

X-ray

yak

zebra

A B C D E F G H I J K L M N O P Q R S T U V W X Y Z

a b c d e f g h i j k l m n o p q r s t u v w x y z

ant

bees

cat

dolphin

elephant

fox

goose

horse

iguana

jellyfish

koala

lamb

moon

nest

A B C D E F G H I J K L M N O P Q R S T U V W X Y Z

a b c d e f g h i j k l m n o p q r s t u v w x y z

owl

vulture

pig

whale

queen

X-ray

radish

yak

sheep

zebra

turtle

unicorn

A B C D E F G H I J K L M N O P Q R S T U V W X Y Z

a b c d e f g h i j k l m n o p q r s t u v w x y z